THE BATTLE OF MONS

Published in the original as Volume 5 of:
The Great War: A Series of Monographs
Using Official Sources

On behalf of the
German Great General Staff

Editors:

Raimund Freiherr von Gleichen-Rußwurm

Hauptmann and Head of the Press Office of the General
Headquarters

&

Ernst Zurborn

Hauptmann on the Great General Staff

Translated into English by:
Robert Dunlop & Holger Puttkammer

Published by Robert Dunlop

ISBN 978-0-9932046-0-9

Table of Contents

Foreword

The monographs in the series *Der große Krieg in Einzeldarstellungen,* appeared as a result of a wartime initiative by the Great General Staff to provide the general public with much greater detail about the battles being fought on their behalf than could be gleaned from a reading the daily army communiqués. Plans existed for approximately forty titles, with provision to add more should this be considered appropriate at a later date. In the event only about thirty percent of these books were actually published between late 1915 and September 1919 when the work came to an abrupt end, halted by the forced disbandment of the Great General Staff under the terms of the Treaty of Versailles. No longer could anything appear under the aegis of the Staff and although the publishing house, Gerhard Stalling, which went on to produce many hundreds of Great War related books, expressed its hope when *Mons* appeared that the hiatus would be temporary, this proved not be the case; this was the final instalment and its publication a stroke of luck for British readers who, collectively, have retained an extraordinary fascination for a battle which was little more than a skirmish in comparison with the titanic Battle of the Frontiers being waged to the south at that time between the French and German armies. It is as well when reading this book to bear in mind that between 20 and 25 August 1914 the French army lost at least 40,000 men killed with many more wounded or missing. Of these, between 25,000 and 27,000 died on 22 August, 7,000 of them in the battle for the Belgian village of Rossignol alone.

Post war, as is well known, the Great General Staff continued to operate secretly under various guises, one of which was the *Reichsarchiv*, which was manned almost exclusively by former General Staff officers. This was the organisation which produced the interwar German military history and strictly controlled access to the massive historical archives, not only those of Prussia, but also of the other contingents which had fought the Great War. Its main concern was the publication, volume by volume, of the official history *Der Weltkrieg 1914-1918*, but such was the scale of military operations that the focus of that massive history was corps level and above. *Mons* gets a few pages in Volume 1 but naturally there is none of the detail contained in the monograph. Furthermore, although as part of the flood of semi-official post war publications intended for the general reader, the *Reichsarchiv* went on to sponsor the thirty six volume series *Schlachten des Weltkrieges*, the entire thrust had changed. The books were not an extension of the series of monographs. Contained within a total of 8,000 pages the deeds of no fewer than 16,500 officers and men were mentioned, because the object then was to emphasise the heroism of the individual confronted by overwhelming odds in an increasingly mechanised war. In other words the aim of German popular military history in the 1920s and 30s was to place the best possible gloss on a lost war and to ensure that the reputation of the old army and, by extension the *Reichswehr*, was maintained and enhanced as much as possible.

As a result, had *Mons* appeared at a later date - and that is far from certain, most of the books published concerned the Eastern Front and other planned 1914 Western Front titles never saw the light of day - it would have been different in tone and detail. In addition, First Army was entirely Prussian so, after the archives in Potsdam were destroyed in an RAF bombing raid in April 1945, it would no longer have been possible to reconstruct the battle from the German perspective. We are doubly fortunate, therefore, to have this account, written by men with full access to the source material. There is a caveat and that is one expressly stated by the General Staff in its introduction to Volume 11, concerned with the early battles in Champagne. 'What these monographs offer is not yet military history'; their point being that it was would take decades for historians with access to all the archives of both sides to produce balanced, objective, work. In many ways we are still waiting one hundred years on. Far too little history of the Great War, especially that produced for the Anglophone audience, often by monolingual historians, takes any account of the German side of the story.

Robert Dunlop and Holger Puttkammer have done the historiography of the war a great favour by making *Mons* available for the first time in English. It tells a familiar story from a different perspective. Read objectively, even bearing in mind the caveat, it should then be impossible to regard Mons as the British tactical triumph it is often portrayed to have been, nor should anybody go on believing ludicrous figures in respect of the casualties allegedly inflicted there on the German army. For too long, as Peter Hart has reminded us in his excellent 1914 history *Fire and Movement*, 'the general approach ... has been to take any high random number and double it.' The only way to dispel ignorance, to move historical enquiry forward, is to exploit all available information. *Mons* is the best account we shall ever have from the German perspective; it deserves a wide audience.

Jack Sheldon

Vercors, France. December 2014

Introduction

On August 23rd 1914, the British Expeditionary Force fought its first major engagement in the Great War. The Battle of Mons quickly found a place in the annals of British military history. Since then, much has been written about the encounter between the British and German forces. The British Official History devoted five chapters to the battle and its immediate aftermath. Several German sources were referenced in the history. Walter Bloem's book was one of the sources. It was translated into English as *'The Advance from Mons 1914'*. Bloem's perspective has been widely re-used in many books about the battle, not least because it supported the anecdotal reports from British regimental histories of heavy German casualties caused by accurate British rifle fire. The translation of von Kluck's memoir has also been popular.

More recently, Terence Zuber made a wider range of German accounts available in English. Zuber's book *'The Mons Myth: A Reassessment of the Battle'* included extracts from infantry, engineer, artillery and cavalry regimental histories. These placed Bloem's account into a broader context, whereby the performance of his regiment was contrasted with the German successes in and around the Nimy-Obourg salient.

2014 marked the 100th anniversary of the Battle of Mons. We took this opportunity to translate *'Die Schlacht bei Mons[1]'*, which was the German official account of the battle. The result provides a fascinating insight into what happened, both operationally and tactically. The effects of the uncertainty about the British are evident. There are

---

[1] 'The Battle of Mons'

several anecdotal accounts from across the battlefront as well. These illustrate how hard the attackers had to work in the face of the British defences, as well as the heroism and determination that opened up those defences in some places. The German decision-making processes are revealed across the different levels of command. This includes details of the various objective lines that limited exploitation when the Nimy-Obourg salient collapsed. Finally, the book includes the German perceptions of the British Expeditionary Force and its performance. We have added some extra maps but have otherwise refrained from adding extraneous text, apart from a few minor points for clarification. Our focus has been to enable the original text to speak for itself.

We would like to acknowledge the support of Dr Jack Sheldon, who not only provided the Foreword but also gave invaluable support and advice. Thanks also to Mick Forsyth, Paul Hederer, Ralph Whitehead, Richard Hargreaves, and Chris Boonzaier, who all helped to make this book into something that we hope the original editors would have been proud of. Finally, we acknowledge the efforts of all those people who have made it possible for us to collaborate together. We are both conscious of the fact that 100 years ago we might have been on opposite sides in the battle. Perhaps the greatest lesson from this book is that we must never let such a battle happen again.

Robert Dunlop and Holger Puttkammer (translators)

[Original] Epilogue

Fourteen monographs have appeared in this series since the autumn of 1915. The work has progressed slowly due to the difficult conditions created by the war. It has not been possible to realize all of the ideas set out in the original scope for the same reasons. Nevertheless, the series has gained many admirers from all walks of life.

It is still necessary to encourage an understanding of the tremendous events that unfolded and to fulfill the desire for detailed accounts of the fighting. The calm associated with the peace process should have made it possible to meet these needs and to continue the process of gradually clarifying the details of the events that took place. With deep regret the General Staff has to stop this work. Under the terms of the peace treaty concluded on 1st October this year, this volume marks the end of the General Staff's remit!

The General Staff wishes to take this opportunity to express its thanks to the publishers. The company constantly and willingly overcame all the difficulties in getting this monograph to print. Hopefully the publishers will manage to continue with the series. It provides an unparalleled record of the heroic battles into which the nation gladly committed the very best of its life and blood!

The Oberquartiermeister for Military History,

Great General Staff,

Berlin, 30th September 1919.

The Advance Through Belgium

(See Map 1. p.74)

The First Army formed the extreme right wing of the German army on the Western Front. Generaloberst von Kluck was the General Officer Commanding (GOC). On 17th August 1914, First Army approached the small Gette river in Belgium. The river presented a potential barrier to the German advance between Diest and Tirlemont (see Map 1a. p.12). Latest intelligence clearly indicated that Belgian forces were still holding that stretch of the river. On the morning of the 17th, General der Infanterie von Lochow, commanding III Corps, was at the eastern edge of St. Trond when Oberleutnant von Witzleben delivered the news that the enemy was defending the river in front of III Corp's march route. Witzleben was the leader of a cavalry patrol from Hussar Regiment 3 that had been sent out to reconnoitre the river. The young Zieten Hussar[2] had been shot in the chest during the patrol and all of the horses had been killed. Despite his severe wound, the patrol leader had made his way back on foot accompanied by some other wounded troopers from his squadron. He had picked up another horse in order to deliver personally the important message about the first encounter with the enemy.

Generalleutnant von der Marwitz, Höherer Kavallerie-Kommandeur 2[3] (HKK 2), had reported on 16th August

---

[2] Husaren-Regiment 'von Zieten' (Brandenburgisches) Nr. 3

[3] 'Höherer Kavallerie-Kommandeur' refers to General von der Marwitz himself and was not synonymous with cavalry corps. The German text does use the term 'Kavalleriekorps' on one occasion for the units under

that the Belgians were entrenched in front of the First Army on the line Diest - Tirlemont – Wavre. At that time, First Army Headquarters was still doubtful whether the enemy would actually defend these positions. Now the hope was that Belgians would still be there the next day, allowing First Army to get round their left flank. The Belgians could then be pushed away from Antwerp and defeated. The orders for the advance on 18th August were issued accordingly.

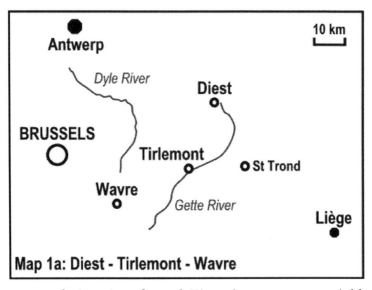

Map 1a: Diest - Tirlemont - Wavre

The general situation forced First Army to act quickly. It was known that the French army was rapidly moving troops north, apparently with the intention of joining forces with the threatened Belgian army. The only information about the British disembarkation was uncertain and contradictory. The one thing that had to be reckoned with was that a British army would arrive on the

---

von der Marwitz's command, which is translated as 'cavalry corps'. Throughout the rest of the translation, however, the acronym HKK is used, in keeping with the original.

Continent in the very near future. It was essential to prevent the assembly of Belgian, British and French reinforcements; otherwise this could spoil the execution of the Supreme Army Command's plan, which was to envelop the main French forces with the strong right wing.

First Army's responsibility, therefore, was to press forward relentlessly and overcome all obstacles that could slow the advance. First Army formed the outer flank or 'rim' of the German Army's wheeling movement through Belgium and France. To the east of First Army, the 'spoke' comprised the German Second, Third and Fourth Armies from west to east. The Fifth Army was located along the line Thionville – Metz and formed the pivot of this movement. The Sixth and Seventh Armies were held back in Lorraine and Alsace.

The hoped-for blow to the Belgian army could not, however, be delivered. King Albert realised that the French and British were not going to fulfill their promises to help. They could not arrive in time to relieve his threatened position. After a short resistance at Diest and Tirlemont, King Albert withdrew his divisions in a series of rearguard actions, first behind the Dyle and then back in a northwesterly direction towards Antwerp. The fighting against the Belgians had caused minimal delay. While screening Antwerp, First Army was able to resume the advance on the following day without major interference.

Under the scorching rays of the August sun, long columns flowed inexorably deeper and deeper into enemy territory. Each column was shrouded in thick white swirling dust clouds from the hard Belgian roads. Any sense of tiredness was overcome by the knowledge of serving a just cause, preserving all that was dear back home and preventing the horrors of war from entering Germany. Indeed, the men were determined to make every effort to overcome the enemy. The traditional German marching and military songs resounded enthusiastically from the ranks. The Army marched as one, bound not only by the usual strict discipline but also by the joy and confidence of victory. It felt like a unified whole, with everyone from the highest commander to the last man full of confidence that, through the hard training in peacetime, they had acquired superiority over all possible opponents. Despite all the devotion to duty, despite the best of intentions, many reservists and Landwehr men could not keep up with the march pace and had to fall out, leaving them downcast and disappointed.

First Army's advance led into the Belgian lowland, which is bounded to the south by the Sambre and Meuse rivers below Namur. An extensive network of good roads, railways and waterways covered the fertile plain. This network helped the movements and resupply of the army significantly. Supply deficiencies did not mean that the troops suffered from shortage of rations. This despite the fact that the railways had been destroyed and that the repair work could not keep pace with the Army's rapid progress. Harvesting had started in mid-July, which meant that enough grain and hay was obtained directly from the fertile, well-cultivated land. Also the highly productive livestock farms furnished plenty of cattle for slaughter. Large scale Belgian horsebreeding helped to replace losses and to maintain the hard strenuous advance of the mounted troops as well as the baggage and supply columns. The extensive copses, woods and other ground cover meant line of sight was considerably reduced throughout the region. This provided valuable assistance to the Belgian defenders. In this part of Belgium, the rural communities and numerous small towns did not have any built-up areas. Homes and industrial buildings were scattered across the countryside, often lining the roads for many kilometres. Fences and hedges surrounded almost all the fields; trees and bushes bordered the streams. This terrain is far from ideal for conventional battle. It lent itself, however, to guerrilla warfare.

IV Corps reached Brussels, the Belgian capital, on 20th August and occupied the city without a struggle. With drums beating, the troops marched past their commander General der Infanterie Sixt von Armin. Thousands of astonished people turned out to witness the rare spectacle. Brussels, the seat of the Belgian government, the intellectual and financial centre of a prosperous country, a city of 650 000 inhabitants, was in German hands - what a huge, highly visible moral victory!

According to press reports received at Army Headquarters on 20th August, the British Expeditionary Force had completed its disembarkation in French ports on 18th August. The direction of the BEF's advance was still unknown, but it had to be assumed that it might close up via Lille (see Map 1b. p.16). As a result, Generaloberst von Kluck saw that his mission had been expanded beyond forming the outer-most wing of the great outflanking manoeuvre. Now he also had to protect the right flank of the German army from the BEF. Von Kluck therefore decided that it would be better for his army to head southwest, with the left flank bypassing Maubeuge. This would put the army in the ideal position to swing south, west or northwest, depending on the direction of the enemy's advance. Second Army

Command, to which First Army and HKK 2 had been subordinated from 17th August for the advance, had a different perspective. They had become convinced that once Second Army turned south then the advance across the Sambre river west of Namur and either side of Charleroi would run into heavy resistance from French forces and that it would not be able to do without First Army's support during these upcoming battles.

On 21st August Generaloberst von Bülow, Second Army commander, therefore ordered the First Army to conform to the movement of Second Army while screening Antwerp. Specifically, First Army was to seal off the north and northeastern approaches to Maubeuge from the area to the west of the fortress in such a way that it could take action to support Second Army if required. Neither Second Army nor the German Supreme Command expected the British forces to come into action in the near future.

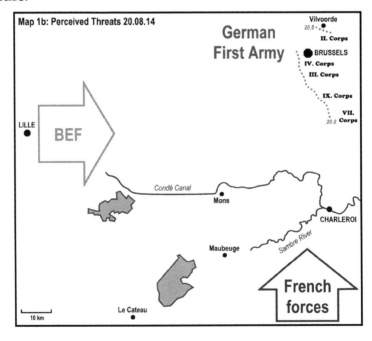

Map 1b: Perceived Threats 20.08.14

The Situation on 22nd August 1914

(Map 2a. p.19)

On the evening of 22nd August, First Army rested east of the line Ninove (II Corps) - Ollignies - Silly (IV Corps) - Thoricourt - Notre Dame Louvignies Road, (III Corps) - Laugenée - Mignault (IX Corps). III Reserve Corps covered the Army's right flank and rearward lines of communication towards Antwerp. Following behind in the second wave, IV Reserve Corps had reached Brussels. The Army Headquarters was in Hal.

In order to preserve the marching ability of the two right wing corps, Generaloberst von Kluck ensured that these corps did not march further than was absolutely necessary. II and IV Corps were therefore not as far forward as III and IX Corps.

HKK 2, who was subordinated to von Bülow's Second Army, had concentrated his divisions (2nd, 4th, and 9th Cavalry Divisions) in front of First Army's right wing, in the area west of Ath.

The forward elements of Second Army began engaging strong enemy forces, part of General Lanrezac's French Fifth Army, on the Sambre River. The fighting had been heavy in places. Second Army's right wing, 13th Division (VII Corps), had advanced from Nivelles towards Binche during the 22nd.

At long last on the same day the veil of uncertainty about what lay ahead of First Army was lifted a little. For the first time came confirmation that British forces had been identified in front of First Army. HKK 2 reported that Cuirassier Cavalry Regiment 2 had encountered a British cavalry squadron at Casteau, approximately 8 km northeast of Mons. The Mons – Condé Canal (Canal du Centre) seemed to be held from Mons to Ville sur Haine. Reports from infantry corps reconnaissance elements confirmed the British presence and that the canal crossings were occupied. Infantry Regiment 26 in the IV Corps sector shot down a British plane that was flying from Maubeuge on a reconnaissance mission to the area west of Brussels.

On the other hand, German planes reported no evidence of the enemy to the west, from the area around Lille west following the railways as far as the Valenciennes - Peruwelz road.

Although British forces lay ahead of First Army, it was still unclear whether these were the main British army or just cavalry and advance guards. In any case, First Army now had to expect that it would come into contact with the enemy somewhere northwest of Maubeuge. From Generaloberst von Kluck's perspective, it seemed even more desirable to create a strong right wing capable of enveloping the British left flank. This desire, however, had to be considered in the context of Second Army's demand. Therefore First Army had to maintain contact with Second Army's right wing in order to support the fighting on the Sambre if needed. Next day Second Army was going to advance east of Maubeuge, with VII Corps proceeding on the right wing from Binche via Solre.

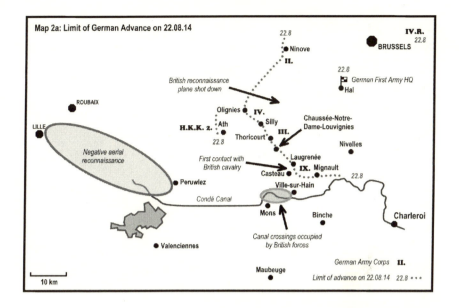

Map 2a: Limit of German Advance on 22.08.14

Generaloberst von Kluck decided to continue advancing towards the area northwest of Maubeuge on the 23rd, while taking measures to protect his left wing from the Maubeuge fortress. In accordance with these plans, the following army order was issued in the evening (see map 2b. p.21):

- II Corps to proceed from Ninove through Grammont to La Hamaide
- IV Corps to Basècles via Ath and Stambruges via Chièvres
- III Corps to St. Ghislain via Lens and Jemappes via Jurbise

The high ground on the southern bank of the canal was to be captured.

IX Corps role was to cover the movement of First Army by screening of Maubeuge. This involved an advance via the line Mons - Thieu towards the north and north-west fronts of the fortress, with most of the force concentrated on the right wing.

IV, III, and IX Corps were to cross the line Ath - Roeulx by 0830 hours next morning. These corps had to reconnoiter as far as: Alost - Audenarde - Renaix - Leuze - Valenciennes - Bavai. First Army's reconnaissance pilots were given the task of checking the area Douai - Cambrai - Le Cateau - Avesnes - Valenciennes.

IV Reserve Corps was to follow up in a second wave. III Reserve Corps continued its role of protecting the right flank from Antwerp. II Corps and IV Reserve Corps were again made particularly aware that Belgian forces were suspected to be in the Alost area.

The message that "the British are ahead" spread like wildfire from corps to corps and man to man throughout the German forces. The troops felt revived at the prospect of getting to grips with this enemy in the next few days; they had become weary with the long marches. Earlier that day the men had joyfully welcomed news of victories in Lorraine and upper Alsace. They felt envious, however, that their colleagues were gathering fresh laurels from these actions. First Army had only fought the Belgians. Most of the time had been spent just marching, constant and unrelenting marching. The men from Holstein, Brandenburg, Lower Saxony and Pomerania looked forward to the coming days with confident enthusiasm.

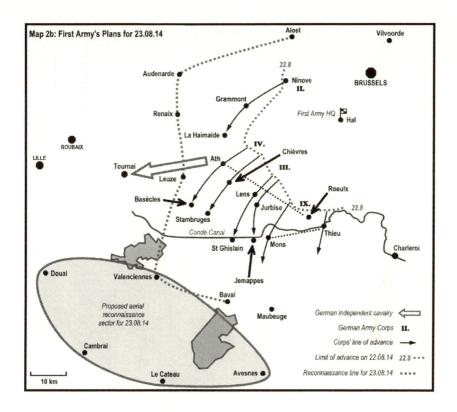

Map 2b: First Army's Plans for 23.08.14

Alost

Vilvoorde

Audenarde

22.8

Ninove
II.

BRUSSELS

Grammont

First Army HQ

Renaix

Hal

La Haimaide

IV.

Chièvres

ROUBAIX

Ath

III.

LILLE

Tournai

Leuze

Basècles

Lens

Jurbise

Roeulx

IX.

22.8

Stambruges

Condé Canal

St Ghislain

Mons

Thieu

Charleroi

Douai

Valenciennes

Jemappes

Bavai

Proposed aerial
reconnaissance
sector for 23.08.14

Maubeuge

German independent cavalry

German Army Corps   II.

Corps' line of advance

Cambrai

Limit of advance on 22.08.14   22.8 • • •

10 km

Le Cateau

Avesnes

Reconnaissance line for 23.08.14   • • • •

21

23rd August.

(Map 2c. p.23)

The Advance and new Intelligence

The early morning of this hot August Sunday saw First Army marching on a broad front in a southwestly direction, in accordance with orders issued the previous evening. The corps spread their divisions along two or more parallel march routes. This meant they were ready to deploy and react to possible contact with the enemy. It would also facilitate crossing the Canal du Centre quickly on both sides of Mons. Only II Corps, which was echeloned back on the right wing, and IV Reserve Corps, which was marching in the second wave, advanced with their divisions on single roads. Every step was taken to reconnoitre the canal crossings. Pontoon bridging equipment was brought forward and incorporated into the marching columns.

The overview of the enemy's dispositions became unclear again. In the morning, the Army High Command in Hal received a message from HKK 2 that a major detraining of troops had been taking place in Tournai, east of Lille, since 22nd August. The continuing, still unresolved question concerning the location of the main British forces became even harder to answer. Given where the British had landed, it was quite possible that they were detraining at Lille. On the other hand British forces had been identified in the Mons area, though only cavalry forces for certain. Aerial reconnaissance in the morning failed to produce any results because of the mist.

First Army continued to advance according to the plan. The army's right flank was protected against the possibility of the British emerging from Lille, with II

Corps being echeloned back and with IV Reserve Corps following on. However, doubt remained if the planned envelopment of the British extreme flank was feasible.

Army Command therefore ordered the lead elements of IV, III and IX Corps to halt, in order to ready the army for a turn to the west. The corps received a specific order not go beyond the Leuze – Mons – Binche road. IV Corps had to specifically cover and reconnoitre towards Tournai as well as maintain contact with HKK 2. After these orders were issued, the Army Command moved to Soignies.

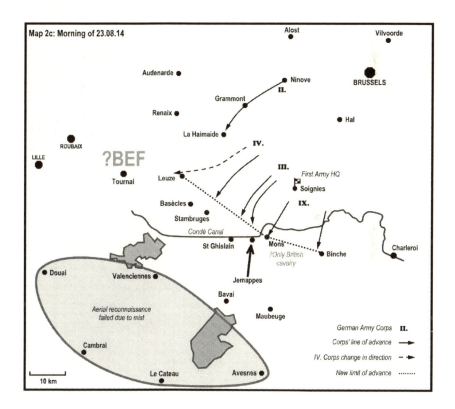

During the morning, more and more messages arrived from the various corps headquarters about the presence of strong British forces in the Mons area. Patrols found that the canal crossings at Obourg, Nimy and St. Ghislain were strongly defended, with weaker enemy units in the villages and woods north of the canal. Local inhabitants told Hussar Regiment 3 that 30 000 British soldiers had been seen on 22nd August marching towards Mons from the area south of St. Ghislain. An intercepted private letter also indicated the presence of a strong British army south of Mons. Second Army's flank 13th Division reported that a British cavalry brigade had been thrown back in a southwesterly direction near Péronnes.

It then emerged that the troops near Tournai were not British but only a French territorial brigade, which apparently belonged to the Lille garrison. The message from HKK 2 had been wrong. This left Army Command in little doubt that stronger British forces would be encountered around Mons and that serious resistance along the canal was likely. The original objectives for the army corps were confirmed again.

Around noon the noise of battle could be heard clearly from the area east of Mons. Elements of IX Corps were engaged in battle at the Canal du Centre. The information was passed on to III and IV Corps, along with the following orders: "III Corps proceed to attack via St. Ghislain – Jemappes; IV Corps advance in the direction Hensies - Thulin to support III Corps." (see map 2d. p.25)

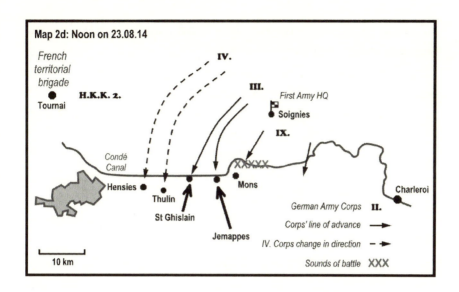

Map 2d: Noon on 23.08.14

The British Army

The British Expeditionary Force (BEF) comprised around 90 000 troops under the command of Field Marshal French. It landed in the French ports of Boulogne and Le Havre. I and II Corps, along with the 1st Cavalry Division, had concentrated in the Maubeuge area by 21st August. The strength of a British infantry regiment was approximately the same as a German battalion.

Field Marshal French was recognized in his own country as an excellent soldier and an admirable leader. He came to prominence as a cavalry general in the Boer War, and looked back on a brilliant military career. I Corps was commanded by General Douglas Haig, who later became the Commander-in-Chief of the British Army on the Western Front. General Smith-Dorrien commanded II Corps and General Allenby led the Cavalry Division.

The assessment of the BEF's fighting value was based on it being made up of volunteers who were veteran colonial soldiers for the most part. The senior officers all possessed a wealth of battle experience from the Boer War. The troops had to be assumed to be courageous, dogged, and expert in field craft. It remained to be seen how their tactical training, which was based mainly on the experiences of the colonial wars, and their leadership would stand up in the grander setting of a European war of movement; they still had to provide the evidence. The well equipped, strongly built soldiers from the allied island kingdom made a great impression on the inhabitants of Picardy, who rightly held high hopes for Field Marshal French and his khaki-clad troops.

Marshal French intended his army to cooperate with the offensive planned for the French Army's left wing, which comprised General Lanrezac's Fifth Army, on 22nd August. The objective was to advance over the Sambre, in the direction of Soignies - Nivelles. The British commander was just as much in the dark as the French High Command about the rapid sweeping advance of von Kluck's army to the north. When General Lanrezac prepared to go on the defensive against the German Second Army behind the Sambre on 22nd August, Marshal French drew up his forces on the high ground around Mons and in a defensive position along the Canal du Centre. The goals were to stop the German advance and to support the French left wing. General French ordered I Corps to defend the area east of Mons and II Corps to defend the canal sector Obourg - Mons - Condé. He sent 5 Cavalry Brigade to link up with the French army's left wing at Binche, while he placed the rest of his cavalry in reserve behind the British left wing thereby condemning them to inaction (see map 2e. p.27). General Joffre, the French Commander-in-Chief, had sent two territorial divisions to strengthen the British right wing but these had not arrived yet.

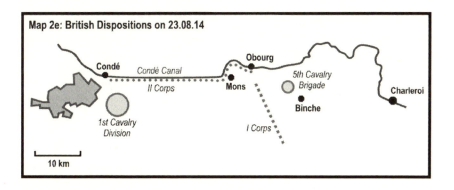

Map 2e: British Dispositions on 23.08.14

The British Defences around Mons

The British defensive position was particularly well chosen. The canal lay directly in front of the line. The area offered natural advantages to the defender but posed enormous difficulties for the attacker. French himself described the position as excellent in his official report[4]. The meadows north of canal were crisscrossed with numerous marshy ditches and barbed wire fences; copses and clumps of trees blocked every line of sight, hindered observation and impaired the effect of the attacker's artillery fire accordingly. What a contrast to the south of the canal where the mining area of the Hainaut region started. East of Mons, the terrain rose in a southerly direction. The hillcrests and the cone-shaped flat-topped slag heaps from the numerous mining operations provided the defender with excellent locations to set up artillery batteries, machine guns and observation posts.

---

[4] The Despatches of Sir John French, 1914.

The British made skillful use of the terrain on both sides of the canal. Trenches had been dug on the forward slopes, barricades built with sandbags and sand-filled barrels, and the houses were loopholed. In contrast, it was clearly evident that the canal bridges were not completely prepared for demolition or destruction. This work was cut short when the British called off their own attack.

Mons' favourable natural position had made the city a central focus for earlier battles. During Caesar's reign, the Romans built a fortified camp there for protection against the *Belgae* tribes to the north; hence the Latin derivation of the city's current name. During the 17th and 18th Centuries, Mons was taken and retaken at various times by the French. Several place names in the neighbourhood were a reminder that the first clash of German and British Armies would take place on ancient historical ground. Even more appropriate, therefore, that the fate of Belgium and France would be decided here. At Malplaquet, south of Mons, Prince Eugene and Marlborough won a victory in 1709, humiliating the French in the War of the Spanish Succession. At Jemappes, southeast of Mons, the French under General Dumouriez defeated the Austrians under the Duke of Saxony in 1792 during the War of the First Coalition[5], which was followed by the French occupation of Belgium.

---

[5] French Revolutionary Wars 1792-1802.

IX Corps' Battle Around Nimy, Obourg and East of Mons

(Map 3. p.76)

Shortly after 0900 hours[6] IX Corps approached the Canal du Centre northeast of Mons in four parallel marching columns. The right column of 18th Division, which comprised the reinforced 35 Brigade, had reached the Champ des Manoeuvres southwest of Casteau at that time. The reinforced 36 Brigade formed the left column, which had reached St. Denis. The 17th Division's reinforced 33 Brigade marched to Ville sur Haine and the reinforced 34 Brigade headed towards Thieu.

Dragoon Regiment 16, half a regiment of which was 17th Division's organic cavalry, reconnoitred ahead and found the canal crossings defended by weak enemy forces. The information was sent back to the division. The artillery was immediately given preference over the infantry march columns and was brought forward into position. The enemy forces, British cavalry, withdrew from the area after a few shots. The dragoons advanced aggressively, easily capturing the intact bridges.

Around 1000 hours, General von Quast (commanding IX Corps) ordered both divisions to advance to the canal crossings. 18th Division's objectives were the bridges between the Obourg-Mons road. 17th Division was directed to the crossings from La Bruyere up to Bracqeugnies. The divisions were instructed not to go beyond the line Nimy - southwest corner of the woods

---

[6] The timings are German, i.e. one hour ahead of UK.

west of the Obourg-Mons road - the southern edge of the Bois d'Havre - Bois du Rapois in the first instance.

The brigades from 17th Division completed the crossing without incident and reached the objective line under the protection of batteries deployed in an overwatch position. 18th Division, however, struck fierce enemy resistance.

Generalleutnant von Kluge directed the right column towards the crossings northwest and northeast of Nimy, while the left column was ordered towards the bridges south of Obourg. All of the artillery was to support the infantry advance. It was positioned along the high ground around Maisieres and southwest of St. Denis.

Opposite 36 Brigade it was discovered that the British had prepared for defence the Obourg railway building located south of the canal and had occupied the edge of the forest running west from there. Further west again, the enemy had expertly entrenched themselves in a position that was difficult to spot. Located about 500 meters northwest of St. Denis, two batteries of 2nd Battalion Field Artillery Regiment 45 opened fire on the bridge area and on the defences that had been detected. Under this covering fire, the men of Infantry Regiment 85 approached Obourg. Third Battalion came under heavy rifle fire from the occupied railway buildings, which prevented any further advance towards the bridge. The batteries were too far back to destroy the obstacles blocking the infantry's advance. The divisional commander ordered an artillery section forward. Despite the intense enemy fire, Leutnant Petersen and two men succeeded in bringing a field gun into position. Unfortunately a house still blocked the field of fire to the British outpost. With a few shots this obstacle was cleared. Several shells were then fired at the other railway building, which soon collapsed in on itself like a house of cards.

Meanwhile, 2nd Battalion (Infantry Regiment 85) succeeded in crossing the canal west of Obourg via a footbridge that was not shown on the map. As a result of the pressure from the troops advancing through the woods west of the Obourg-Mons road on the far shore, the enemy fled headlong from Obourg bridge. Third Battalion Infantry Regiment 85 and 2nd Company Engineer Battalion 9 were able to exploit this success by capturing the bridge intact, despite the fact that demolition charges had been prepared. 1st Battalion Infantry Regiment 85 was called forward, along with the attached battalions and other elements of Infantry Regiment 31. They deployed to attack the British, who were defending a prepared position in the hills northwest of Mons.

35 Brigade halted on the road from Casteau, its leading elements having reached the Champ des Manoeuvres, in order to await the arrival of the results of the reconnaissance of the Canal. Returning patrols reported that the enemy had occupied the crossings near Nimy. At 1030, the Brigade's GOC, Generalmajor Hunäus, ordered 3rd Company Engineer Battalion 9 and the two battalions marching in the vanguard of Infantry Regiment 84 to capture the crossings northwest of Nimy. At the same time, the bulk of Fusilier Regiment 86 was to turn south and take the lock bridge located halfway between Nimy and Obourg.

Fusilier Regiment 86 deployed in Obourg Wood with two battalions leading followed by one battalion and the Machine Gun Company. This force worked its way forward to the southern edge of the forest. Moving quickly, the riflemen took the building occupied by the enemy north of the canal. The enemy fled back across the canal. The Fusiliers came under heavy fire from the far bank of the canal during the pursuit, which prevented them from getting closer to the canal crossing. Once Field Artillery Regiment 9 had put some hits on the buildings south of the canal, several brave men were able to cross the weir gate and lower the raised bridge. The rest of the regiment then crossed the canal, penetrating into the enemy's positions on the far bank and capturing numerous British soldiers. Shortly after 1400 hours the regiment halted their advance on the objective line, which was the hill on the southwest corner of the forest west of the Obourg-Mons road. 2nd Battalion was despatched to the right flank towards Nimy, where the brigade's sister regiment was engaged in a fierce battle and could not advance.

After crossing the Champs des Manoeuvres and traversing the forest north of Maisières, two battalions of Infantry Regiment 84 were held up by fierce resistance in front of the canal just north of Nimy. At the same time, 3rd Battalion Infantry Regiment 85 had already run into the enemy in Maisières and had followed up the enemy's fighting withdrawal to Nimy. 3rd Battalion Infantry Regiment 85 was then held up there by heavy enemy fire. 11th Company had suffered heavy casualties, whilst 10th Company lost its company commander, Hauptmann Stubenrauch, two platoon commanders, and a large number of NCOs and ORs. The regimental commander, Oberst von Amelunxen, then pushed 2nd Battery Field Artillery Regiment 9 forward. They provided strong support to 2nd and 3rd Battalions Infantry Regiment 84, whereupon Lieutenant Gerling distinguished himself with his platoon by successfully gaining a foothold in the northern outskirts. The enemy, however, continued to resist strongly from the trenches along the edge of the canal. It was not until 1430 hours that the enemy gave way under the pressure of the well aimed supporting artillery fire from the northern canal bank. Subsequent patrols found that the railway bridge west of Nimy had been blown up and the swing bridge northwest of the town had been swung round to the southern canal bank. Musketier Niemeyer from Sergeant Röwer's patrol (8th Company Infantry Regiment 84) boldly dived into the water, swam across the canal and collected a boat, which the patrol used to cross over despite being under heavy fire. While Sergeant Röwer and his men on the bridge kept up suppressing fire on the enemy, Niemeyer succeeded in swinging the bridge back again, so that the rest of the company was able to get across. Niemeyer died heroically as soon as he had completed this brave deed.

Oberst von Amelunxen now went forward personally to the head of the regiment, which then crossed the bridge and stormed the southern side of the canal sector near Nimy. All three battalions became involved there in a tough struggle to clear the occupied houses and barricades in the streets. Despite the opposition of the residents, who actively supported the British, the regiment succeeded in penetrating through to the southern edge of the burning village in about 30 minutes. The brigade gathered there, reorganised and got ready to push forward. Looking around the British defensive position revealed their heavy losses, both dead and wounded.

By the early afternoon, all of 18th Division had successfully crossed the canal, even though some units had taken significant losses[7]. Even before the divisional commander received news that Nimy had been captured, IX Corps ordered him to take Mons and push on to the objective line Cuesmes-Mesvin. At the same time 35th Brigade was directed towards Mons and 36th Brigade was committed towards the high ground east of the city.

Generalmajor Hunaeus ordered Infantry Regiment 84 to capture Mons and Mont Eribus, located south of the city. He ordered Fusilier Regiment 86 to maintain contact with Infantry Regiment 84 and to push forward east of Mons.

After a strong officer's patrol determined that the area north of Mons was clear of the British, at 1830 hours Oberst von Amelunxen formed up Infantry Regiment 84 and despatched its leading elements towards the city centre. Morale was high as a result of the victory. The men of 1st and 3rd Battalions Infantry Regiment 84 started singing patriotic songs. They crossed the main square in front of the proud old town hall without incident. As the advance guard approached the tightly packed 2-3 storey houses along the winding roads to the south of the city, it suddenly came under heavy machine gun and rifle fire. The regiment and brigade staff horses following behind the point guard turned around and raced back, initially causing confusion when they collided with the following column. The advance stopped and an alternative route was sought. The reconnoitering patrols then came under fire in the side streets. Lieutenant von Köller, the regimental orderly officer, rushed back to Nimy and brought forward a section of Field Artillery Regiment 45. The guns were unharnessed and brought forward, protected by their shields. The houses known to

---

[7] '*nicht unerheblichen Verlusten*' in the original text, i.e. 'not insignificant casualties'.

be occupied were shelled, which ended the enemy's resistance in short order. They quickly evacuated the city in a southerly direction. Mons was ours! Mont Eribus was occupied at 2000 hours. 2nd Battalion Infantry Regiment 84 circled around to the west side of Mons discovering that railway installations had been destroyed.

At dusk, 35 Brigade bivouacked along the line Mont Eribus – Hyon, the latter town having been occupied by Fusilier Regiment 86 without a fight. The line at the final limit of the advance was consolidated, outposts were set up, and liaison with 36 Brigade was established on the left.

36 Brigade had met fierce enemy resistance on the northeast side of Mons but had stormed the enemy position with great courage in the evening, capturing 3 British officers and 202 other ranks as well as 4 machine guns. The retreating enemy was threatened on his western flank by elements of 17th Division at St. Symphorien. During the evening, the brigade rested in battle readiness along the Mons - Obourg road, where 18th Division's Staff was also located. All along the 18th Division frontage close contact was maintained with the enemy, particularly with the enemy outposts on the southern slope of Mont Eribus.

The 17th Division had found only a few small enemy units defending the canal in the morning, which meant it pushed forward in the afternoon and reached Villers St. Ghislain and Saint Symphorien without much resistance. Late in the afternoon, the division became involved in fierce fighting with the British, who were occupying the high ground south of Malplaquet and southwest of Villers St. Ghislain. By 1730 hours 33 Brigade, intending to try and cut off the retreat of the British forces east of Mons, who were opposing 18th Division, set off from Bois d'Havre and Saint Symphorien towards Mons – Hyon. However, Infantry Regiment 76 could not get beyond the high ground on the western edge of St Symphorien because Infantry Regiment 75 and 2nd Battalion Field Artillery Regiment 24, echeloned on Infantry Regiment 76's left flank, became engaged with the enemy at Malplaquet.

Infantry Regiment 75 was uncertain initially about whether the men entrenching in Malplaquet and the columns observed on the roads were friend or foe. Inbound enemy artillery fire soon made it clear, as did recognition of the brown uniforms of the British infantry. The leading battalion, 3rd Battalion Infantry Regiment 75, deployed but experienced significant losses from artillery fire while crossing the St Symphorien – Villers road. 2nd Battalion Infantry Regiment 75 was deployed on the left of 3rd Battalion Infantry Regiment 75. The battalions worked their way forward by bounds just like on the parade ground. The machine gun company deployed on the left wing of the regiment and established itself in a wooded area. From there it was able to bring effective fire to bear on the enemy line. 10th Company Infantry Regiment 75 got to about 100 metres from the enemy. 9th and 12th Companies followed, along with 2nd Battalion Infantry Regiment 75, until heavy enfilade fire forced them to stop. Without any regard for the danger, officers and NCOs rushed forwards. Following their example and the encouraging cry, "Fix bayonets!" everyone hurled themselves forward again. The regiment's commander, Oberst Jaeger[8], seeing what happened, decided to order 1st Battalion Infantry Regiment 75, which was following

---

[8] Oberst Jaeger was wounded at Nampcel on 20 September 1914 and died of his injuries.

behind the left wing, to extend the front line laterally. The battalion worked its way up to 2nd Battalion Infantry Regiment 75. The riflemen approached to within 200 - 300 metres of the enemy positions, but then had to wait for nightfall before attempting another advance. During the night, an officer's patrol probed forward and detected considerable movement in and behind the enemy lines. The conclusion was that the British were being reinforced in order to attack the next morning. The regiment, which no longer had any reserves and had become severely disorganised during the battle, was withdrawn back to the high ground around St Symphorien. The Bremen regiment [i.e. Infantry Regiment 75] lost 5 officers and 376 men killed and wounded in the attack.

In the evening, 34 Brigade positioned two battalions of Fusilier Regiment 90 to the left of Infantry Regiment 75, covering the enemy from the high ground southwest of Villers. The riflemen worked their way forward in the darkness until they were about 500 metres from the enemy. The rest of the brigade reached Villers St. Ghislain and the high ground about 1 km south of the village without making any enemy contact. Field Artillery Regiment 60 was located south of Villers. It maintained a lively exchange with enemy artillery until dusk.

Fighting dismounted, Dragoon Regiment 16 chased off an enemy cavalry squadron on the left flank at midday. By evening, the regiment was south of Bray.

The staff of 17th Division stayed at Villers St. Ghislain.

III Corp's Battle Around St. Ghislain and Jemappes.

(Map 3. p.76)

General von Lochow assigned two march routes to his army corps for the 23rd August. The 5th Division was to proceed from Thoricourt towards St Ghislain via Lens and Baudour. The 6th Division's objective was the high ground south of Jemappes. To get there, Generalleutnant von Roydon needed to take the main road from Chaussee Notre Dame de Louvignies to Mons, turn west at Masnuy St. Pierre, and then to turn south via Jurbise through the big woods northwest of Mons. The canal posed a major obstacle to the advance of both divisions northwest of Mons. The divisional commanders requested that officers of the engineer companies from the Spandau Battalion[9] should accompany the Hussar Regiment 3 reconnaissance patrols to explore the condition of the crossings. It was not possible, however, to get to the bridges to examine them. No matter how they tried to wind their way through the numerous farmsteads scattered between the villages of Tertre, Ghlin and Nimy, they came under fire from hidden infantry. The cavalrymen tried to parallel the roads but endless barbed wire, hedges and wide ditches contrived to stop even the boldest hussars. One patrol was reduced to two hussars on a bridge northwest of Mons. Leutnant der Landwehr Müller, the engineer officer accompanying them, went missing.

By 1100 hours, 6th Division's advance guard had almost crossed the huge forest near Ghlin and was approaching the village with its numerous barns, stables and other farm outbuildings. The commander, Generalmajor von Gabain, was still uncertain about what lay ahead. He began dispersing his forces to avoid leaving the protection of the forest in column of march. Just then a message arrived;

---

[9] This is a reference to Pionier-Bataillon von Rauch (1. Brandenburgisches) Nr. 3 - garrison town Spandau.

the enemy had evacuated Ghlin but was occupying Jemappes. When the point guard reached Busteau Station north of Ghlin, a corps order arrived at about 1100 hours from General von Lochow in Tirbise. The order required the III Corps to form up along the line Tertre – Ghlin in readiness for an attack on St. Ghislain - Jemappes. According to the army order, once the units were deployed then they had to wait in their assembly areas. Not until a III Corps order devolving freedom to manoeuvre once more arrived at 1500, could a start be made. Infantry Regiment 64 was moved up alongside Infantry Regiment 24, the existing advance guard regiment. The 12 Brigade objective was Jemappes. Infantry Regiment 20 followed up, echeloned further back on the left. Not long after the infantry had set off, Field Artillery Regiment 3 and the howitzer detachment of Field Artillery Regiment 39 opened fire on Jemappes, the railway station and the bridges.

The 1st Battalion advanced quickly along the Ghlin - Jemappes road, on the right flank of Infantry Regiment 24. After a brief skirmish in the gardens and farms north of the canal, the battalion approached the north bank of the canal. It was now impossible to advance any further. The enemy opened a murderous fire. They were well-entrenched and completely hidden from the assault troops between houses on the far bank.

East of the Ghlin - Jemappes road, the advance of 2nd Battalion Infantry Regiment 64 was considerably more difficult. The lines of infantry worked their way forward painstakingly through the dense tangle of wire fences and hedges, jumping and wading through the network of ditches. Under the overcast August sky, the oppressive midday heat lay heavily on the meadows of the marshy low-lying Belgian countryside. There was not a breath of wind to cool sweating limbs. Burning thirst tormented the men as they pushed forward, gasping under the burden of knapsacks and ammunition pouches. The advance continued steadily up to 900 meters from the steep canal wall. Then suddenly the canal bank on the far side came alive. Just single shots to begin with, then rapid rifle fire, followed by machine gun fire and British artillery batteries sending their first greetings. It was time to work forward by bounds, exploiting every bit of scarce cover and gaining ground by crawling forward. Still nothing could be seen of the enemy. The top of the canal embankment was targeted as the suspected location of the enemy infantry. Losses increased. Bounds forward became shorter. Finally the whole advance stalled.

As a result there was a wide gap between 1st and 2nd Battalions Infantry Regiment 24. 3rd Battalion Infantry Regiment 24 was following 1st Battalion Infantry Regiment 24 through the streets of Ghlin. Oberst Freiherr Prinz von Buchau therefore ordered 3rd Battalion to send two companies to plug the gap and to seize the bridge about 800 metres east of the Ghlin - Jemappes road bridge. 3rd Battalion Infantry Regiment 24 began its approach from the fork in the road about 400 meters north of Jemappes. The objective was clearly visible. The bridge seemed to be raised but undamaged. 2nd Engineer Company had tried already to seize the crossing by surprise but was repulsed immediately with bloody losses. Infantry Regiment 24 also failed, just as the engineers had, despite a section of guns from Field Artillery Regiment 3 being pushed forward and keeping the rows of houses on the canal under fire.

Meanwhile, an artillery section from the Brandenburg Regiment[10] came into action at point blank range in support of 1st Battalion. Thanks to the accurate fire of the two guns, Hauptmann von Altrock and his men, who had taken cover alongside the Ghlin road, rushed forward and captured the crossing. The 1st Battalion companies followed and forced their way south of the canal into Jemappes. The enemy ceased resistance and fell back. Infantry Regiment 64 followed 1st Battalion Infantry Regiment 24 across. Eventually 2nd and 3rd Battalions Infantry Regiment 24 reached the captured bridge.

General von Gabain was able to re-organise his brigade that evening on the high ground south of the town.

Generalleutnant von Rohden intended to capture the high ground near Frameries and south of Cuesmes by the end of the day. He marshaled his brigades in the direction of Frameries - Ciply at about 2000 hours: 12 Brigade on the right and 11 Brigade to the left. The objective could not be reached, however, because of the chaotic terrain with numerous railway installations, factories and slag heaps. When night fell, most of 6th Division halted along the line of the Quaregnon - Flenu - Cuesmes railway. Picquets were pushed forward only a few hundred yards to protect the exhausted troops.

Fifth Division's day was even harder fought.

After a march of about 30 km via Lens - Herchies, the vanguard of Grenadier Regiment 12 arrived at Baudour village on the southern edge of the wood of the same name. Here they were able to close up and get some rest. The field kitchens drew up and were quickly surrounded

---

[10] This is a reference to Feldartillerie-Regiment General Feldzeugmeister 1. Brandeburgisches Nr. 3.

by the companies. When each man's mess tin was full, he stretched out his tired limbs in the roadside ditch and ate his meal in complete comfort. It seemed to the grenadiers, however, that the rest of this day would, like so many others recently, be taken up just with marching. The men welcomed the chance to rest because the long march and the intense heat had been exhausting. Suddenly everyone was on the alert, listening intently! The sound of rifle fire could be heard close by, off to the southwest.

Suddenly hussars returned and reported that the troopers had come under fire approximately 2 km ahead in Tertre. Both Tertre and the canal at St. Ghislain appeared to be heavily defended. Leutnant von Münch, a platoon commander from 10th Company Infantry Regiment 12 that had secured the station south of Baudour, recognized British cyclists in Tertre. Immediately Major Prager, the ever-energetic commander of the Fusilier [3rd] Battalion, asked permission to clear Tertre with the help of a field gun. A gun from Field Artillery Regiment 54 was quickly brought forward. British soldiers could be seen running to the rear as soon as the first shot was fired. Leutnant Münch and his men rushed forward and forced their way into the village, followed by the gun. It had to be used several times in amongst the houses and then the platoon reached the southern edge of Tertre. Major Prager hurried forward as well, followed by his battalion. On the southern edge of the village the Fusiliers came under heavy fire from a group of houses about 900 meters further along the road towards St. Ghislain. Major Prager ordered the leading company, 10th Company Infantry Regiment 12, and the next two: 12th and 9th Companies Infantry Regiment 12, to capture the houses. He was then hit by a bullet and killed. Right next to him Leutnant

Grapow, commander of a platoon of the Machine Gun Company, also fell. When artillery fire began falling in Tertre from the far canal bank, there was no longer any doubt that at long last stronger enemy forces lay ahead.

Meanwhile the regimental staff received a divisional order to capture the bridges at St. Ghislain. Oberst von Reuter pushed 1st Battalion Infantry Regiment 12 forward west of Tertre and sent the rest of the Machine Gun Company to support the Fusiliers. Hauptmann von Stocki took a platoon from 12th Company Infantry Regiment 12 and succeeded in clearing a substantial farm, which had been the source of particularly heavy fire. Hauptmann von Stocki was killed soon afterwards. Once 1st Battalion, leaving Tertre to its left, had worked its way through the dense undergrowth of the wood and with 2nd and 3rd Companies in the lead, had drawn level with occupied groups of houses, the enemy stopped resisting.

Oberst von Reuter recognised, however, that the two battalions would not be enough to attack the enemy holding the canal. Second Battalion Infantry Regiment 12 had just reached the northern edge of Tertre. Reuter therefore ordered the battalion to bypass Tertre to the east and then attack on the left of the Fusilier [3rd] Battalion. After 2nd Battalion had arrived and the 5th and 8th Companies had drawn level with the Fusiliers, the advance began all along the line. The battalions had to attack across a broad flat battlefield, intersected with ditches and wire fences. Beyond the level ground of the green meadows rose a dark, continuous line - the embankment of the Canal du Centre. The enemy could not be seen, which meant that Field Artillery Regiment 54 was unable to provide effective fire support for the infantry from their position southeast of Tertre. The

Grenadiers and Fusiliers were enthusiastic about closing on the British and finally bringing well-aimed fire to bear on them. Competing with one another, the companies and platoons pushed forward aggressively, paying no attention to the rapidly increasing losses from mainly British machine gun and shrapnel fire tearing into their ranks. The support platoons were quickly used up and the reserve companies had to launch forward vigorously.

Meanwhile Leib-Grenadier Regiment 8 from 9th Brigade went into action to the east of Grenadier Regiment 12. At 1515 hours, the division commander had ordered the regiment, which was waiting north of Douvrain, to attack the railway and road bridges at Mariette to support Grenadier Regiment 12. It advanced with 1st Battalion on the right, Fusilier [3rd] Battalion on the left, and 2nd Battalion echeloned left in the second line. Dispersed skirmish lines were formed so that the fields north of Mariette could be crossed without attracting fire. The houses north of the canal were reached and found to be free of enemy forces. The riflemen continued to push through the built-up area towards the canal. Suddenly they came under heavy rifle and machine gun fire from the buildings on the opposite bank. It seemed that especially strong defensive positions had been established in the houses near the bridges. The battalion commanders realized that it would be impossible for the infantry acting alone to advance further. Major von Johnston of the Fusilier [3rd] Battalion, therefore, contacted 1st Battalion Field Artillery Regiment 18 and asked for two guns. A section from 1st Battery under Lieutenant Mierendorff succeeded in getting forward and opening fire. A house alongside the canal crossing was soon reduced to rubble. The brigade commander, General von Doemming, was with the Fusilier [3rd] Battalion and ordered the 10th Company to assault. They pushed forward but were brought to a standstill when heavy fire broke out again. Fusiliers and gunners together manhandled the guns even further forward. Shot after shot was then fired at point blank range at the loopholes in the building. The few shells that the section had brought forward were quickly used up. Wachtmeister Trampe succeeded, with the greatest coolness, to bring an ammunition wagon to the guns just in time. Shelling was resumed and effectively silenced the enemy's fire briefly. Exploiting this opportunity, elements of both battalions simultaneously reached the canal in several places. The Fusiliers advanced over the road bridge. Hauptmann von Sichart and the 10th Company got across using a makeshift crossing beside the bridge and then advanced east of Mariette. In Mariette itself, the fighting for the houses and barricades went back and forth, with elements of both battalions quickly becoming mixed together. At around 1700 hours, the Leib-Grenadier Regiment was in complete control of Mariette.

Grenadier Regiment 12's attack on St. Ghislain did not achieve its objective. The companies of 2nd Battalion were stuck a few hundred metres short of the canal, the fusiliers had worked their way forward astride the road to a point about 400-500 metres from St Ghislain, 6th and 8th Companies were barely 200 metres from the enemy trenches which had now been located, whilst 5th was still about 700 metres short. Friendly fire had almost totally died away. The severely reduced lines of riflemen lay almost clinging to the ground, just as though they were determined at all costs to hold on to what they had achieved. Each man saved his last few rounds, either to be

45

ready to exploit a favourable opportunity or to meet an enemy counter-attack. Many dead and wounded grenadiers lay in the broad meadows that had been crossed during the attack. The dressing station in Tertres could barely keep up with the work. With a heavy heart, Oberst von Reuter realised that his regiment had almost bled to death and, deciding that he could not in all conscience be responsible for the further sacrifice that a renewed final attempt would bring with it, decided against any further advance for the time being. Instead, he passed an urgent request to the sister arm to ease the situation of the grenadiers through increased fire and thus make the attack possible.

Neither the divisional nor the brigade commander was in ignorance of the tremendous difficulties being experienced by Grenadier Regiment 12 in its battle. As a result they had already set in train measures to assist the regiment, timed for the very moment when Oberst von Reuter had given up as hopeless the prospect of capturing the crossings. Infantry Regiment 52, the brigade reserve regiment on standby in Tertre, had already received orders in the early afternoon to prolong the right flank of 1st Battalion Grenadier Regiment 12 and met them by deploying its 2nd Battalion. 5th and 6th Companies, together with a platoon of the Machine Gun Company, which made up the first line, were greeted by rapid fire from unseen enemy from the direction of the canal and the right flank. It was then spotted that the enemy, too, had extended their western flank. As a result the battalion commander, Major Behr, also deployed 7th Company with two machine guns, despatching them in the direction of La Hamaide. About 4.30 pm the regiment was ordered by division to capture the canal crossings about 1,200 metres southeast of La Hamaide. By those means, General Wichura[11] hoped, finally, to relieve the pressure on Grenadier Regiment 12. This intention was further reinforced by a second order to Infantry Regiment 52, which was already in action, to swing east once the bridges had been taken and so assist Grenadier Regiment 12.

Infantry Regiment 52 now fought its way forward southwards towards the bridges; 1st Battalion astride the La Hamaide - Haine railway and 5th and 7th Companies either side of the Petit Villerot - Haine road. The presence of houses lining the roads, farm houses, farm buildings and gardens gave the battles the feel of street fighting. Intimate support by a gun of 1st Battery Field Artillery Regiment 54 under Oberleutnant Neumann made it possible for the battalion to close up swiftly to a point about 200 metres short of the canal. Here it succeeded in cutting off 72 men of the Yorkshire Regiment and capturing them. This, however, brought the first assault of the 52nd to a standstill.

Whilst the attempt was being made by the brigade reserve regiment to the right of Grenadier Regiment 12 to assist in the battle for St Ghislain, further to the left the Leib-Grenadier Regiment [Grenadier Regiment 8] which had successfully forced a crossing at Mariette, set about supporting its comrades from the Frankfurt garrison[12]. The mission of the 1st Battalion was to advance on St Ghislain, having traversed Mariette and swung west. This was achieved and it closed up on Hornu without coming

---

[11] Commanding 5th Infantry Division

[12] This is a reference to the fact that Grenadier Regiments 8 and 12 were both stationed in Frankfurt an der Oder in peacetime.

under fire. A cycle patrol sent forward was shot down in the centre of that place, so elements of the battalion set out to attack Hornu, whilst others moved against St Ghislain, which was occupied by the British. The attack did not get forward and did not, therefore, produce the desired relief. The other two Leib-Grenadier battalions now turned from Mariette towards Wasmuel and occupied this town at 2000 hours. Darkness prevented any further advance in the confused terrain of slag heaps.

After the artillery had done its utmost to prepare for the attack, Oberst von Reuter ordered a general advance of his Grenadier Regiment on St. Ghislain at 1830 hours. Several companies heroically tried again but they were forced to a standstill by the increased ferocity of fire raining down from the canal embankment and from the houses in St. Ghislain. Other companies could not even launch forward; any attempt to do so being foiled by the alert enemy machine-gunners. Command and control broke down because all the runners were killed or wounded while trying to reach the front lines. The regimental commander finally decided to call off the attack and elected to wait for the cover of darkness before attempting to cross the canal. As night fell officer patrols, probing forward, discovered such a strongly occupied enemy position that it was decided that the attack should be postponed until early next morning. The assault was coordinated with the artillery. Wiskott's Battery from Field Artillery Regiment 54 was moved forward and went into position next to the Fusilier Battalion in the centre of the infantry regiment.

The warm summer night enfolded the blood-soaked battlefield of the 12th Grenadiers, and the darkness provided protection from enemy fire. The company commanders looked for their platoon leaders, who in turn searched for their men. By this time several Leutnants had taken over the posts of Hauptmann or Oberleutnant, while many NCOs were attempting to recreate platoons. The infantry who were furthest forward, whose fearless attempt had stalled so close to the objective, were pulled back to create a continuous front in case there was a surprise counter-attack from the tough enemy.

The casualty lists revealed that 25 officers and more than 500 NCOs and ORs had sealed their loyalty in death or who, wounded, had to be withdrawn from the ranks.

The enthusiasm with which the men had gone into battle at noon, despite the strenuous march earlier, gave way to a sombre and melancholic mood. The men were well aware that they had done their duty but the heavy losses and the general feeling of a missed victory weighed heavily on everyone's minds. It was not until the next day that the attack turned out to have not been in vain.

The Brigade Regiment had more luck and had finished fighting by the late afternoon. The mission of relieving the Grenadiers after dark, however, could not be carried out. At 2030 hours, 1st and 2nd Companies of the 52nd stormed the railway bridge south of La Hamaide while singing "Deutschland, Deutschland über alles". The enemy had carried out a demolition on the bridge but this did not stop 2nd Company from crossing over and taking up a protective position on the far bank. During the night, patrols of the 3rd Company along with engineers under the command of Hauptmann Pehlemann, Engineer Battalion 3, reached the road bridge. They found that the bridge was undamaged and that the enemy had withdrawn. The bridge was captured.

Generalleutnant Wichura remained with his staff in the station building at Tertre. At 2100 hours he issued the order for the division to rest in the positions that had been reached, ready to renew the attack at daybreak.

IV Corps

(Maps 2. & 5. pp.75 & 78)

III Corps' heavy fighting for the bridges around St. Ghislain and Jemappes prompted Generaloberst von Kluck to set IV Corps on the move in the afternoon once more. Its mission was to capture the southern canal bank and thereby support III Corps. IV Corps had already received an order at 1400 hours to march towards Hensies and Thulin but this had been postponed by a subsequent army order to stop and rest.

After a march of nearly 40 km, 8th Division had reached the outskirts of Basècles via Ath - Ellignies and 7th Division had reached the area of Stambruges via Brugelette - Beloeil.

The 8th Division was assembled again in the vicinity of Grandglise (2½ km north of Harchies) at around 1830 hours in order to march to Hensies via Harchies.

At the same time 7th Division started marching again, heading via Ville Pommeroeuil to capture the canal bridges en route to Thulin. The advance guard under Generalmajor Schüßler's command made contact with the British after passing through Ville Pommeroeuil. The British were holding the railway embankment south and southeast of the village. Infantry Regiment 26, supported by 1st Battalion Field Artillery Regiment 4 deployed by the Bois de Ville. They quickly attacked the railway embankment, ignoring the lively enemy shrapnel fire, and then attacked west of the road to Thulin towards the canal. At this point the attack came to a standstill because the enemy kept the area north of the canal under constant machine gun fire. General von Schüßler then deployed a battalion from Infantry Regiment 66 on the left of the Infantry Regiment 26. Infantry Regiment 66 reached the canal at 2110 hours but could not go on because the enemy fire continued unabated. At around midnight a makeshift footbridge was completed successfully despite the enemy machine gun fire. First to cross over the shaky planks to the far bank was Leutnant von Reuß with NCOs and men from 10th Company Infantry Regiment 26. Leutnant Schacht followed behind with a machine gun platoon. After temporary repairs had been made to the bridge the enemy had blown, 3rd and parts of 1st Battalion were able to cross under the cover of night. 2nd Battalion Infantry Regiment 26 and 2nd Battalion Infantry Regiment 66 were ferried across on pontoons from the divisional bridging train. The 26th and 66th entrenched themselves either side of the roadway, about 400 metres south of the canal. The uncertain situation and the darkness ruled out an immediate continuation of the attack. When 8th Division's advance reached the southern exit of Harchies, fierce house-to-house fighting broke out between the Machine Gun Company of Infantry Regiment 93 and the British. Hauptmann Thümmel, the company commander, fell in the heroic onrush while leading his men from the front. Leutnant Freiherr von Ledebour was also killed, having urged his men on to greater efforts with the words "Above all, victory must be ours". After eliminating the resistance, the advance guard commander pushed 2nd Battalion Infantry Regiment 93 on towards the enemy-occupied northern-most canal crossing on the Harchies - Hensies road. The battalion soon captured the bridge with the support of 2nd Battalion Field Artillery Regiment 74 and then continued on to attack the southern bridge. However, Infantry Regiment 93's forward progress was halted by heavy rifle and machine gun fire from farm buildings on the far bank. It was not possible to continue the attack because of nightfall and the lack of artillery support. The British blew up the bridge during the night.

The Situation on the Evening of 23rd August and the Plans for 24th August.

(Map 2. p.75)

When evening came on August 23rd, First Army's engaged corps were fighting along the general line of the canal from north of Hensies - 1km north of Thulin - north of St. Ghislain - the southern edge of Mons – to St Symphorien. II Corps was positioned behind the right wing at La Hamaide west of Lessines. IV Reserve Corps had reached Bierghes behind the army's centre.

Heavy gunfire could be heard from the east in the late afternoon, indicating that Second Army was still engaged in battle. VII Corps had thrown back the enemy to its front. The corps' right wing had reached Binche and was to continue the attack towards Merbes le Chateau[13] on 24th August.

As the various actions unfolded throughout the day, it became clear that First Army had engaged strong British forces. The defence had been tough, especially against III

---

[13] 18 km east northeast of Maubeuge and 10 km south of Binche.

Corps. It was likely that the enemy would take advantage of the high ground south of Mons and would continue to resist strongly next day.

Whilst the situation to the front had been clarified as a result of the battle, Army Headquarters was still totally unclear about what was happening on the right flank. HKK2 was operating to the right of First Army from the area from Ath in a northwesterly direction across the Scheldt to Courtrai and had not encountered any enemy forces. There was no more news from the area further south, where detraining had been observed around Lille in the morning, nor from Tournai where French infantry had been noted at midday. The presence of other hostile forces, British or French, still had to be reckoned with. Nevertheless it seemed that there was no imminent danger to the army's right flank; it was even hoped that the extreme enemy flank lay to the front.

Generaloberst von Kluck decided to continue the attack the next day against the enemy force to his front, enveloping its left wing. The aims were to prevent the enemy from disengaging to the west and to push them towards Maubeuge. The front line army corps were given axes of advance for a general half right sideways move, in order to avoid bunching up towards Maubeuge. At the same time, IX Corps was to screen the northwest front of the fortress. II Corps was to reach Condé by a night march so as to participate in the envelopment of the enemy flank. In its place, IV Reserve Corps was to move behind the right wing and to protect against any surprises from the west. This corps' objective was Ligne, west of Ath.

HKK2 was tasked to proceed southwest in the general direction of Denain. The mission was to clarify the situation on the army's right flank and to prevent the enemy from retreating west. General von der Marwitz was subordinated to First Army on the evening of the 23rd so that Generaloberst von Kluck could direct the cavalry corps.

24th August

A fine drizzle was falling during the early morning of 24th August as the battle-ready troops of First Army anticipated the coming day. Now and then the sound of a gun firing, either from the enemy's or from the German artillery, broke the stillness of the dawn. Gradually the firing became heavier. Rifle fire was heard, along with several staccato bursts of machine gun fire. At 0500 hours, fighting began again almost simultaneously all along the front.

IV Corps at Elouges and Audregnies.

(Map 5. p.78)

In IV Corps, only 7th Division had succeeded in getting larger detachments across the canal during the night. Dawn reconnaissance patrols from 8th Division found that the British had evacuated the southern bank of the canal. After 3rd Company Engineer Battalion 4 had prepared some crossings, the rest of the men formed up at about 0900 hours to advance on Hensies. Following the sudden alarm on the previous afternoon, the infantry regiments were not marching in their correct brigade formations. Therefore on the 24th, Infantry Regiment 93 and Infantry Regiment 72 combined as Brigade Reichenau; whilst Infantry Regiment 153 and Infantry Regiment 36 formed Brigade Duke of Altenburg. After Infantry Regiment 72 had captured Quiévrain without difficulty, Brigade Reichenau, supported by Field Artillery Regiment 74, went into battle with the enemy on the line

Marchipont-Audregnies just after 1300 hours. Brigade Altenburg had remained back southwest of Hensies to protect the open right flank. It was now given the mission to wheel south, skirting north of Crespin, to envelop the enemy's left wing.

Brigade Reichnau's attack pushed forward quickly, although the infantry repeatedly came under very effective British artillery fire from the northern side of Audregnies. At 1400 hours, 1st and 2nd Companies Infantry Regiment 72 suddenly forced their way into Audregnies. The British artillery had just enough time to limber up; three ammunition wagons were left behind. Even the last minute British cavalry charge towards Audregnies did not stop the German infantry from penetrating into the town. The advance continued on and reached the line of the high ground southeast of Marchipont, south of Audregnies. The enemy retreated in a southerly direction. Further pursuit was called off to avoid being pulled in the wrong direction. The army's objective of enveloping the British meant marching southwest, not south.

Brigade Altenburg reached Quiévrechain without encountering any serious resistance.

From 7th Division, 3rd Battalion Infantry Regiment 66, led by its brave and tireless commander Major Knauff, crossed the line Haine - Bach at 0500 hours. After a short struggle, it overwhelmed the small garrison that was staunchly defending Thulin. Reserve Leutnant Borchert, leading elements of 8th Company, distinguished himself by his dash and determination. The advance halted on the line of the Valenciennes - Mons railway. Infantry Regiment 26 reached the same line, but off to the right. After a short halt along the embankment, the division received an order from General der Infanterie Sixt von

Armin at 1100 hours. The attack was to continue towards the high ground near Elouges, where the enemy had been located. 13 Brigade was to proceed on both sides of the Thulin – Elouges road, deploying a strong right flank to drive the enemy southeast if possible. The 41 Brigade was to follow, echeloned behind the right wing.

At around 1320 hours, 1st and 2nd Battalions Infantry Regiment 66 moved off on the western side of the Thulin - Elouges road, with 3rd and 1st Battalions Infantry Regiment 26 on the eastern side. Widely spaced skirmish lines were used to make the push towards the heights of Elouges. The enemy tried in vain to stop the attack with shrapnel. The battalions rushed forward without any pauses. They were well supported by the artillery under General von Stumpff's command, positioned behind the railway embankment. The enemy lines were smothered with well-timed shrapnel fire and the enemy artillery was silenced. The British did not wait for the attack to reach them. They abandoned their positions and retreated hurriedly in a southerly direction, pursued effectively by our fire. After passing through Elouges, the advance halted at the Elouges - Quiévrain railway embankment. Only Infantry Regiment 26 suffered significant losses as a result of the fierce fighting amongst the farms and slag heaps.

British resistance was broken surprisingly quickly in IV Corps' sector. The infantry gratefully acknowledged the brilliant collaboration of their own artillery, which contributed significantly to the success. Morale was high and the troops were fired up for further action. Significant numbers of prisoners, machine guns and horses were brought in. For example, 600 British troops surrendered when Elouges was taken.

IV Corps rested up in the evening, with 8th Division in the area Quiévrechain - Baisieux – Quiévrain and 7th Division in and around Elouges.

III Corps at Hornus, Wasmes, Paturages and Frameries.

(Map 4. p.77)

General von Lochow arrived near Flenu at about 0600 hours. He took up position on one of the towering slag heaps there. The confusing terrain, numerous buildings, factories and mines made it very difficult to exercise control of the battle. During the night, the general had ordered the 5th Division to occupy St. Ghislain and then deploy south of Hornu facing southwest. The 6th Division had to be ready at 0400 hours for further action on the high ground near Frameries.

Both divisions began moving again as ordered.

On 5th Division's right wing, 1st and 2nd Battalions Infantry Regiment 52 set off in the direction of Boussu and Hornu towards 0500 hours, having crossed the captured bridges during the night. 2nd Battalion Infantry Regiment 48 followed them. At the same time, artillery fire was directed onto the crossings near St. Ghislain again. The enemy evacuated the bridges, and Infantry Regiment 12 was then able to reap the rewards of its previous day's attack. 3rd Battalion Infantry Regiment 52, which had been placed at the disposal of Oberst von Reuter, was first across the bridges near St. Ghislain and then advanced towards Hornu. The Grenadiers followed behind.

Both regiments became entangled in a fierce battle south of Hornu, where the enemy had established another position that was defended tenaciously. The trenches were well sited, making best use of the terrain to cover the front and flanks. The slagheaps, which dominated the whole area, were occupied, providing significant extra support.

The Leib-Grenadier Regiment was advancing east of Hornu when it encountered the enemy in a position to the north and northwest of Wasmes.

At 1425 hours, Generalleutnant Wichura ordered his division to attack. 10 Brigade was to support 9 Brigade, which in turn was to support the 6th Division attack. The boundary between the brigades was the line running from the southern exit of Hornu to Champ des Sarts.

There were major difficulties getting the artillery forward over the canal but this was the key to get the battle flowing. Field Artillery Regiment 18 went to the west of Quaregnon, 2nd Battalion Field Artillery Regiment 54 took up a position to the right. 1st Battalion Field Artillery Regiment 54 was brought further forward to the fork in the railway line between St Ghislain and Wasmuel. 3rd Battery was pushed even further forward and brought down outstanding fire for effect against two enemy batteries in particular.

After the infantry had got to within about 400 m, the enemy abandoned his positions at 1500 hours and withdrew to the south.

6th Division, which had spent the night on the high ground south of Jemappes, concentrated all its artillery in the early morning against Frameries and the neighbouring buildings, bringing them under heavy fire. Recent experience had shown that close quarters fighting in built-up areas demanded strong artillery support to avoid heavy losses. Field Artillery Regiment 39 fired from positions south of Flenu and Field Artillery Regiment 3 from the area east of Flenu station.

The infantry launched their attack at around 0830 hours. 12 Brigade was tasked with attacking Frameries. On the brigade's right, Infantry Regiment 20 worked its way towards Paturages. The British fought back desperately. They were hidden amongst the numerous industrial buildings and mining infrastructure. Their rifle fire often took the attacking regiments in enfilade, causing significant damage. Nothing, however, could diminish the advancing Brandenburgers' resolute will to win. This determination initially enabled 1st Battalion Infantry Regiment 24 to assault the northern side of Frameries and eject the enemy from his position. The same energy also drove 1st Battalion Infantry Regiment 64's advance against the high ground near Frameries' graveyard, which was doggedly defended. Despite heavy enemy artillery fire, Major Matthiaß was able to reach and then clear the enemy from two successive lines of trenches. Infantry Regiments 24 and 64 reached the Paturages - Noirchain road around noon. Simultaneously, Infantry Regiment 20 was also able to reach this line by infiltrating Paturages, which was in flames in several places. The enemy withdrew.

General von Luchow now gave the order for the two divisions to proceed in the direction of Warquignies. 5th Division had to form up in the area south of Hornu, with 6th Division operating in support towards Eugies. There was no further fighting, however, because the enemy finally seemed to have given up resisting. Operations were halted at around 1800 hours, with 5th Division settling down for the night around and to the north of Dour and 6th Division around and to the north of Warquignies. Patrols from Hussar Regiment 3 were sent towards Bavai and further west in order to maintain contact with the enemy.

IX Corps

35 Brigade of 18th Division had been supported by Field Artillery Regiment 45 during the night when in close proximity to the enemy on Mont Eribus, while 36 Brigade with Field Artillery Regiment 9 subordinated had pushed south of Hyon as far as the area around la Trouille. As dawn broke, it was roused by the sound of rifle fire, giving the impression that the enemy had been reinforced - something which seemed to be confirmed when, shortly afterwards, the enemy artillery also opened up with heavy fire.

Generalleutnant von Kluge halted his staff at the Mons - St. Symphorien / Mons – Malplaquet fork in the road and surveyed the battlefield. General von Quast also arrived shortly afterwards at 0500 hours.

Corps headquarters learned from 17th Division that it had not had any further contact with the enemy during the night or in the morning.

At that, the corps commander designated the divisional boundaries for the further advance, directing them, however, not go beyond the Noirchain - Givry road because of the threat from the Maubeuge fortress. No sooner had the order been despatched at about 0900 hours than a pilot reported that the line Ciply - Nouvelles

- Givry was held only by weak infantry and artillery in delaying positions. Numerous small columns were seen retreating south and southwest between Bavay and Valenciennes. The pilot confirmed that the enemy's artillery at Givry, Nouvelles and Frameries was engaged in an intense firefight with our own batteries.

The enemy fire slackened off suddenly at about 1000 hours. There was no more resistance to the advancing infantry, who found that the enemy had apparently marched off in great haste. Several knapsacks and heavy British overcoats were lying about, thrown away by their owners to avoid disaster.

At 1400 hours, General von Quast received a message from III Corps about its favourable progress near Frameries. VII Corps indicated that it was already engaged in combat near Merbes St. Marie, south of Binche. At around 1545 hours, the GOC IX Corps ordered his corps to shift right in order to protect III Corps from Maubeuge. The divisions were to follow each other along the Frameries - Eugies - Sars la Bruyère road towards Ruinsette. There were delays in getting the divisional marching columns into line, so that the corps' leading elements had only reached Eugies by the evening. Outposts were set up at Sars la Bruyère to protect the rest of the troops.

The Situation on the Evening of the 24th and the Plans for 25th August.

(Map 2. p.75)

First Army Headquarters estimated the strength of the enemy that had been engaged so far at 2-3 divisions.

During the day the enemy put up strong opposition to III and IV Corps but had then retreated under the First Army's strong pressure from the direction Curgies - Bavai. The picture of the enemy's situation was rounded off by captured British and French orders. It seemed likely that the whole British Expeditionary Force would accept battle in the area between Valenciennes and Maubeuge. HKK 2 had dispersed a French infantry brigade at Tournai but had not encountered any stronger enemy forces. For the time being, therefore, there seemed to be no danger to the army's right wing.

Second Army indicated that it had decisively beaten the enemy opposing it that day and that they were pressing the victorious attack.

Generaloberst von Kluck hoped to strike the decisive blow against the British army during the following day. He therefore ordered the continuation of the attack for August 25th. IV and III Corps were to cross the line Onnaing - Angres - Athis by 0500 hours. IX Corps was to screen off the attack from Maubeuge and provide support to III Corps as the situation dictated. II Corps, which had occupied Condé during the day, was to sweep through Raismes Forest and southwest of Valenciennes towards the enemy left flank. IV Reserve Corps, which had also reached its objective (the town of Ligne) during the day, would move out via Basècles in time for the advance guard to reach Condé at about 0900 hours morning and then be available to the Army commander.

General von der Marwitz was given the mission of getting the cavalry behind the British and cutting off their retreat to the west.

The British

On 22nd August the British army received news from General Lanrezac's French Fifth Army on the right flank that the French position was not safe. They had been hit by a major German attack on the Sambre and had been forced to pull back. General Lanrezac had had to turn to the British Commander-in-Chief and to beg him to push forward on the right flank of the French Fifth Army against the German threat. Marshal French believed, however, that he could not comply with this request because of the German forces advancing towards him. The British commander was desperate to get accurate information about the strength and direction of the advancing German army units in front of him but this had not been forthcoming. He decided therefore to make a stand next day behind a frontal defence, while also maintaining the option of pushing forward to relieve the French Fifth Army. The British commander seemed unconcerned about his left flank because he only assigned the cavalry division to provide protection.

On the morning of 23rd August the British II Corps stood along the canal line Obourg - Mons - Condé. 3rd Division had occupied the angle projecting northeast of Mons. The divisional right wing was bent back sharply to link up with I Corps, which was deployed in echelon to the rear. 19 Brigade was still marching up from Valenciennes.

Field Marshal French apparently harboured doubts that the position occupied by his forces could be held. In particular, the wide north-facing salient formed by the curve in the canal northeast of Mons seemed to him to be vulnerable to an attack. He therefore arranged for a second defensive position to be established along the line Frameries - Paturages - Wasmes - Boussu.

The first German attack (18th Division) was indeed launched against the salient formed by the canal between Obourg and Nimy. The attack put the brave companies of the 4th [Bn] Middlesex Regiment and [4th Bn] Royal Fusiliers in a very difficult position, causing the reserves of the Royal Irish Rifles to be committed hastily. Despite excellent support for the infantry from the artillery located south of Mons, the defensive position was lost by 1500 hours. The British 3rd Division fell back through Mons and Hyon with heavy losses. 9 Brigade was able to re-establish a position southeast of Mons, whereas 8 Brigade was deemed by the British to be no longer battle-ready.

Meanwhile, fierce fighting also erupted west of Mons. The British 5th Division had a hard time from the attack by III Corps. Nevertheless, the division managed to hold its ground temporarily around St. Ghislain against the attack of Grenadier Regiment 12, which was pressed with the utmost gallantry. The East Surrey Regiment was holding an advanced position northwest of St. Ghislain. The battalion only just escaped complete annihilation by hastily pulling back across the canal. The news of 3rd Division's retreat caused 5th Division to fall back on the second prepared position. A strong rear guard remained in the original line, while the divisional main forces reached the rear position just after dark.

Field Marshal French received updates from his commanders about the outcome of the fighting along the canal. Additional intelligence arrived from other sources as well. As the information came in, the overall situation appeared to him to become more hopeless with each passing hour. By the afternoon, the French Fifth Army had already sent a detailed assessment of its desperate situation. General Joffre, the French Commander-in-Chief, confirmed the threat of encirclement in a telegram that evening. According to these reports, the British were facing three German corps to the front, while II Corps was bearing down from Tournai towards the British left wing as well. The Germans had thrown back the French Fifth Army and had forced the crossings over the Sambre between Namur and Charleroi. Furthermore, Field Marshal French could not count on any significant French support for the British left wing. He abandoned any last thought of going over to the offensive and decided to pull back his army to the previously reconnoitered line Jenlain - Maubeuge to avoid the risk of total defeat of his army. He told II Corps to withdraw towards the area east of Bavai. I Corps was given the mission of covering II Corps' retreat in the vicinity of Givry. The Cavalry Division and attached 19 Brigade were to provide left flank protection to II Corps.

It was extremely difficult to disengage the two divisions of II Corps. They were involved in heavy fighting with the enemy at close quarters. Commander 3rd Division ordered the Northumberland Fusiliers and 1st Battalion Lincolnshire Regiment to occupy Frameries. The Oxford[shire and Buckinghamshire] Light Infantry Regiment was ordered to hold Paturages for as long as possible, while the K[ings] O[wn] Yorks[hire] Light Infantry, Royal Welch [sic. 'West'] Kent, Bedford[shire], and Duke of Wellington Regiments had to make a stand in Wasmes.

14 and 15 Brigades of 5th Division took up positions during the night north of the Mons - Valenciennes

railway, along with 19 Brigade under General Allenby's command. The brigades fell back on Quiévrain and Thulin in the morning, under heavy pressure from IV Corps. The Cavalry Division provided support, being hit hard in the fighting near Audregnies and Elouges.

3rd Division, supported by a brigade from I Corps, put up a dogged resistance but had to abandon Frameries, Paturages, and Wasmes around noon. I Corps then withdrew to the area east of Bavai without major losses.

The whole British Expeditionary Force was in full retreat as the day drew to a close. The day's actions had resulted in significant casualties and had caused the regiments to become very mixed up. The hasty retreat had become a complete mess. The situation in Bavai was a shambles. Leaderless companies pushed their way through streets that were clogged by transport of every description. The staff officers tried as hard as they could to bring some order to the general chaos.

When Field Marshal French and his staff were in Bavai, information reached him about the French Fifth Army's defeat on the Sambre, and the embattled French Third and Fourth Armies on the Meuse. To make things worse, news about the threat to the British left flank was increasing by the hour. French realised that the position between Maubeuge and Valenciennes was untenable and he decided to retreat further to the line Le Cateau - Cambrai.

25th August

(Map 2. p.75)

First Army Headquarters spent the night in Soignies. The fresh intelligence arriving during the night gave the impression that the British were attempting to fall back on Maubeuge. The messages gave no indication, however, of how disordered the enemy was.

At around 0800 hours, Generaloberst von Kluck ordered the army to change heading and advance in a southerly direction. The aim was to cut off the retreat of the British army and the French left wing.

The assumption underlying these orders, however, proved to be wrong during the course of the morning. According to reliable reports, the main enemy forces were between Bavai and Le Cateau with a weaker contingent retreating southwest via Solesmes.

The enemy had to be caught and then forced to give battle. With this in mind, IV Corps was re-directed with its right wing on Solesmes while II Corps advanced further to the west. General von der Marwitz was ordered to get his cavalry divisions into contact at all costs and to pin the enemy. IX Corps' role was to screen the northwestern front of Maubeuge; IV Reserve Corps was to advance via Valenciennes.

Overall, however, it was not possible to get to grips with the enemy during this day. General von der Marwitz threw back French territorial troops near Bouchain and forced British columns northwest of Solesmes to turn in a southerly direction instead of retreating towards Cambrai. 8th Division IV Corps came into contact with hostile forces at Solesmes in the evening. The enemy put up a stubborn resistance and was only forced out of the village during the night.

Generaloberst von Kluck and his Chief of Staff, Generalmajor von Kuhl, worked tirelessly to maintain the pursuit of the beaten enemy. Their personal example fired up the staff and troops to do their very best. These senior commanders motored to the heads of the army columns, which were striving indefatigably to push forward. They arrived in Solesmes early on the 26th, only a few hours after the enemy had left the town.

First Army's order for 26th August demanded equally great feats of marching to prevent the enemy from resting. The pursuit needed to press in a general southwesterly direction, with the right wing via Cambrai, the left wing via Le Cateau, and IX Corps continuing to screen the French fortress of Maubeuge.

Closing Remarks

Engagements like the Battle of Mons seem small and insignificant compared to the major battles that occurred later in the war in the West, East and South. Even smaller when compared to the enormous battles of 1918, where individual armies wrestled on the field to bring about a military decision but all the people and all the industries of the world were involved in the struggle for survival versus complete oblivion. The Battle of Mons may be considered as a mere prelude to the great events that for over four years caused the world to hold its breath. We have grown accustomed to the enormity of what has happened, focusing only on the sheer scale of the massed violence. In this light, the soldierly virtues of individual performance and leadership appear under threat. Machines seem to be the decisive factor, rather than personal courage and self-sacrifice. It is doubly important, therefore, to look back over the great achievements of our glorious army. It set out in August 1914, buoyed up by the affection and enthusiasm of a united country and accompanied by the hopes of those left behind. Neither misplaced confidence in victory nor haughty arrogance inspired the whole of Germany as its Army in the West advanced. Rather there was resolute determination, coupled with anxiety about whether the army would cope with the superior numbers of the combined French, British, and Belgian forces. There was also the worry about large parts of the army preparing to take on the Russian masses. The quick fall of Liège and the first successful battle in Lorraine certainly provided a boost. These early victories confirmed that German soldiers were willing to fight and die, and that the German command was equal to the task through its skill and willing acceptance of responsibility. But would these facts count for anything when faced with overwhelming odds?

The news of the first victory over the British relieved the initial fear and anxiety.

Let there be no doubt that First Army won a "victory" over the British, no matter how much they try to play down the German successes. It was a victory, even though it did not decide the outcome of the war and even though the number of prisoners and captured trophies does not stand out to the untrained eye. To appreciate the true level of success all the circumstances have to be taken into consideration, particularly what happened as a result.

The British commander himself stated in his dispatch that the "very heavy ['serious' in the original text] losses, which the British Forces have suffered in the [this] great battle," were attributed to the fact "that the British Army – only two days after a concentration by rail – was called upon to the withstand a vigorous attack of five German Army Corps". This is the best proof that Generaloberst von Kluck did the right thing in forcing the enemy to accept battle on August 23rd.

The British commander succeeded in withdrawing in time from the hoped for encirclement. The pell mell nature of the retreat caused the troops' mental stability to waver, however, more so even than the effect of the significant numbers of killed, wounded, and captured. Consequently Field Marshal French was never again able to organise his forces to mount a vigorous resistance. On 26 August the British army only just escaped total destruction at Solesmes - Le Cateau, which prompted French to note this as "the most critical day"[14] in his despatch.

The French High Command was about to assemble an army detachment in Lille under General d'Amade to support the British left wing. The British defeat and withdrawal prevented the detachment from concentrating according to schedule. The individual formations were defeated separately in detail by First Army on 27, 28 and 29 August respectively.

The left wing of the French army had been engaged by Second Army on 20 to 24 August near Charleroi and thrown back. In the aftermath, the British army was unable to protect the left flank. This meant that the French 5th Army was beaten again on 29 and 30 August in the Battle of St. Quentin.

The success of the Battle of Mons was not based on the battle alone. There was no doubt about the German infantry's excellent achievements: the 12th Grenadiers, the Leib-Grenadier Regiment, the 84th and other regiments. Their "*Friedenschule*[15]" passed the test at Mons with flying colours. The daring of the gunners and the courage of the cavalry on reconnaissance were superb, paving the way for the attacking infantry. Victory, however, was not simply gained on the 23rd when the enemy's resolve to stand fast was broken, nor on the 24th when the British rear guard was broken. Victory had already been set in place by the speedy implementation of First Army's sweeping operations, by means of which the plan for cooperation between the allied Belgian, British, and French armies was foiled. The unexpected advance and

---

[14] Refers to the sentence "Although [General Sordet] rendered me valuable assistance later on in the course of the retirement, he was unable for the reasons given to afford me any support on the most critical day of all, viz., the 26th."

[15] A reference to peace-time military training.

the ruthless attack enabled the individual enemy armies to be caught out during their deployment and disrupted. Marshal French, meanwhile, had already given up the prospect of victory when he chose to make a stand at Mons, thereby handing over the initiative.

The German army's extraordinary marches enabled Generaloberst von Kluck and his commanding officers to succeed. It needed a special force to perform such achievements – an army that had become accustomed to march discipline in peacetime, which had trained to overcome every physical demand and in which reservists and men of the Landwehr almost equaled the performance of the regulars from the very beginning. Only such a force could have initiated the Battle of Mons and won.

Map 1: Situation on 20.08.14

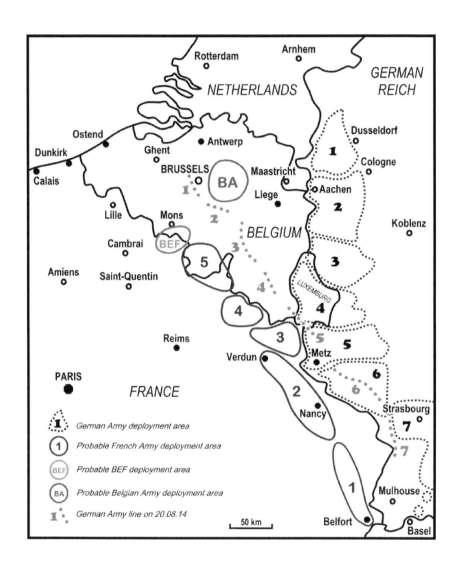

German Army deployment area

Probable French Army deployment area

Probable BEF deployment area

Probable Belgian Army deployment area

German Army line on 20.08.14

50 km

Map 2: Overview of First Army's Operations

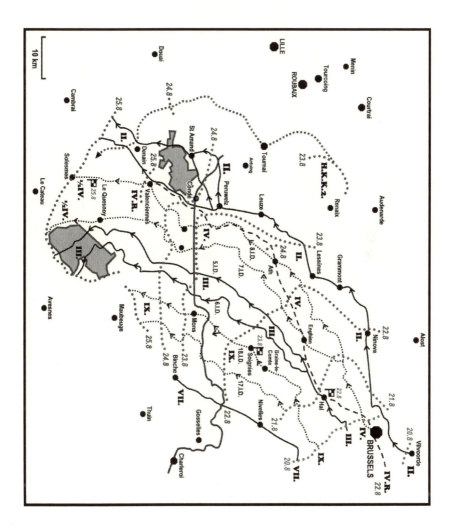

Map 3: IX Army Corps Battle on 23 & 24 August

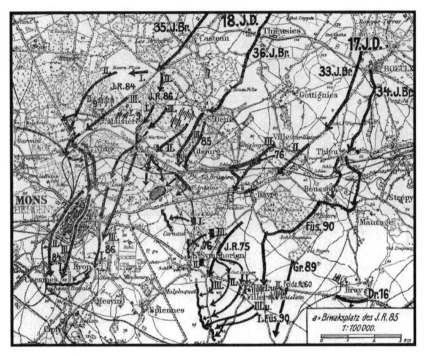

Translators' notes:

- *'J.D.'* is the abbreviation for infantry division.

- *'J.R.'* is the abbreviation for infantry regiment.

- *'Biwaksplatz des J.R. 85'* is the bivouac site for Infantry Regiment 85. The area is marked with a hatched oval about 3 km west of Mons.

Map 4: III Army Corps Battle on 23 & 24 August

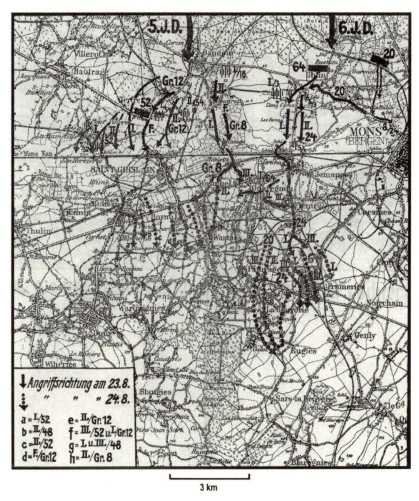

Translators' notes:

- *'Angriffsrichtung am...'* refers to the direction of attack on the specified date.

- *'J.D.'* is the abbreviation for infantry division.

Map 5: IV Army Corps Battle on 23 & 24 August

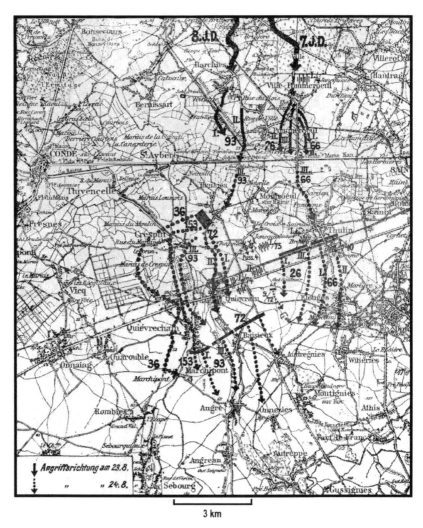

3 km

Translators' notes:

- *'Angriffsrichtung am…'* refers to the direction of attack on the specified date.

- *'J.D.'* is the abbreviation for infantry division.

Order of Battle for First Army in August 1914

Army Commander: Generaloberst von Kluck

Chief of Staff: Generalleutnant von Kuhl

IV Reserve Corps

Corps Commander: General der Artillerie von Gronau

Chief of Staff: Oberstleutnant von der Heyde

7th Reserve Infantry Division: General der Infanterie Graf von Schwerin

22nd Reserve Infantry Division: General der Infanterie Riemann

III Reserve Corps

Corps Commander: General der Infanterie von Beseler

Chief of Staff: Oberst Meister

5th Reserve Infantry Division: Generalleutnant Voigt

6th Reserve Infantry Division: Generalleutnant von Schickfuß und Neudorff

IX Army Corps

Corps Commander: General der Infanterie von Quast

Chief of Staff: Oberstleutnant Sydow

17th Infantry Division: Generalleutnant von Bauer

18th Infantry Division: Generalleutnant von Kluge

IV Army Corps

Corps Commander: General der Infanterie Sixt von Armin

Chief of Staff: Generalmajor von Stocken

7th Infantry Division: Generalleutnant Riedel

8th Infantry Division: Generalleutnant Hildebrandt

III Army Corps

Corps Commander: General der Infanterie von Lochow

Chief of Staff: Oberstleutnant von Seeckt

5th Infantry Division: Generalleutnant Wichura

6th Infantry Division: Generalleutnant Herhudt von Rohden

II Army Corps

Corps Commander: General der Infanterie von Linsingen

Chief of Staff: Oberst Freiherr von Hammerstein-Gesmold

3rd Infantry Division: Generalleutnant von Trossel

4th Infantry Division: Generalleutnant von Pannewitz

H.K.K.2

Senior Cavalry Commander: Generalleutnant von der Marwitz

Chief of Staff: Major von Waldow

2nd Cavalry Division: Generalmajor Freiherr von Krane

4th Cavalry Division: Generalleutnant von Garnier

9th Cavalry Division: Generalmajor von Bülow[16]

27th mixed Landwehr Brigade: Generalleutnant Dallmer

11th mixed Landwehr Brigade: Oberst von der Schulenburg

10th mixed Landwehr Brigade: Oberst von Lenthe

---

[16] Killed at Louvigny on 6 August 1914. Replaced by Generalmajor Graf von Schmettow on 7 August.

Made in the USA
Coppell, TX
23 April 2024

31636975R00049